Past Praise for Sarah Sarai

On *That Strapless Bra in Heaven*

"Astoundingly witty, intelligent, playful poems. . . . So many of Sarai's poems end with a witty twist that makes the dizzy logic of what precedes seem so perfect."

— CHARLES RAMMELKAMP, *COMPULSIVE READER*

"She opens us up to the dignity of surviving when our rulers seem out of control and selfish, and this is an important lesson for now and truly for all of human history."

— JOHN BRANTINGHAM, *CULTURAL WEEKLY*

"If you're also in a carpe diem mood or ready to reassess what you think about luck, the nature of God, or what it means to be famous or frightened or the owner of anything, this is a good volume of poems to read right now."

— JEANNE GRIGGS, *NECROMANCY NEVER PAYS*

"It seems that she's writing for those of us who have gathered in the speakeasies of our world. And can't get out."

— ALEXIS QUINLAN, *HEAVY FEATHER REVIEW*

On *Geographies of Soul and Taffeta*

"Her poems are acrobatic, so her remembering the reader is generous, since making it easier for the reader makes the poet's work harder."

— MARY MERIAM, *THE BIND*

More on *Geographies of Soul and Taffeta*

"Her poems acknowledge the human capacity for boundary — and our inability to come to terms with fallibility. And while the poems speak to intimacies, to a constellation of personal intimacies that do the world a service in being global, they also speak to a state of people in crisis. Of people steering into the sun, unsure how they even got in the car in the first place, and where they'll go next."

— JULY WESTHALE, *LAMBDA LITERARY*

"Even angels here — and there are a few — are pretty pedestrian, waiting at the bus stop with the rest of us, nursing their own doubts or, in any case, presenting particular problems for description: 'a lingering phosphorescence, no / luminescence, oh! it is incandescence.'"

— SPENCER DEW, *DECOMP*

On *The Future Is Happy*

"Her optimism is undergirt by a restless intelligence, a hardheadedness about the world, and a willingness to be vulnerable."

— JEE LEONG KOH, *SONG OF A REFORMED HEADHUNTER*

"Sarai makes an unabashed assault on despair. . . . The confrontation and interactions with an emotional life give these poems a nervy, discomfiting vitality. Their very rawness and urgency bring these poems to a kind of transcendence."

— G.E. SCHWARTZ, *GALACTEA RESURRECTS*

More on *The Future Is Happy*

"Sarai is sexy, funny, philosophical, gracious, and irreverent — sometimes all in the same poem. . . . But in the end, it is not her eclectic subject matter or her charming, sassy style that will win the reader over — it is her willingness to, without artifice or pretension, offer her truth to the page."

— MELISSA STUDDARD, *AMERICAN BOOK REVIEW*

Bright-Eyed

Also by Sarah Sarai

That Strapless Bra in Heaven
Hemet, California: Kelsay Books, 2019

Geographies of Soul and Taffeta
Brooklyn, New York: Indolent Books, 2016

The Risen Barbie
New Shoreham, Rhode Island: Dusie & Forsootharian Press,
    2015

O You of the Cotton Pajamas!
New Shoreham, Rhode Island: Dusie Press, 2014

Emily Dickinson's Coconut Face
New Shoreham, Rhode Island: Dusie Press, 2013

I Feel Good
Oak Park & Chicago, Illinois: Beard of Bees Press, 2013

The Future Is Happy
Kenmore, NY: BlazeVOX Books, 2009

Bright-Eyed

Sarah Sarai

POETS WEAR PRADA • Hoboken, New Jersey

Bright-Eyed

Poets Wear Prada
533 Bloomfield Street, Second Floor
Hoboken, New Jersey 07030
http://pwpbooks.blogspot.com

Publication Credits (ix, x) constitute an extension of this copyright page.

First North American Publication 2024
First Mass Market Paperback Edition 2024

PUBLISHER'S CATALOGING-IN-PUBLICATION DATA
Names: Sarai, Sarah, author.
Title: Bright-Eyed / Sarah Sarai.
Description: Hoboken, NJ: Poets Wear Prada, 2024.
Identifiers: LCCN: 2024931049 | ISBN: 978-1-946116-28-4 (paperback)
Subjects: LCSH American poetry—21st century. | LGBTQ+ people—Poetry. | LGBTQ+ people—Biography. | California—Biography. | Autobiographical poetry. | BISAC POETRY / American / General | POETRY / LGBTQ+ | POETRY / Subjects & Themes / General | BIOGRAPHY & AUTOBIOGRAPHY / Memoirs | YOUNG ADULT NONFICTION / Poetry
Classification: LCC PS3619 .A73 B75 2024 | DDC 811.6—dc23

Printed in the U.S.A.

Front Cover Image: chromolithograph of paper lantern (c. 1880), anonymous, from 19th-century maker's catalog, published in Kircheim-Teck, Germany, The Metropolitan Museum of Art, The Eliasha Whittelsey Collection.

Author Photo: a selfie, Sarah Sarai, 2022.

For my parents.
Who broke with the East.
Who moved us west.

And mixed with these were splashes of California poppies. These too are of a burning color — not orange, not gold, but if pure gold were liquid and could raise a cream, that golden cream might be like the color of poppies.

— JOHN STEINBECK, *EAST OF EDEN*

Table of Contents

Publication Credits

The author extends her gratitude to editors of the following journals or books in which these poems, some in earlier versions, appeared:

Anti-Heroin Chic	"Finery in the Aisles"
The Café Review	"Two-Story Bldg. on Vernon"
Chaotic Merge	"In a Yard in Southern California"
The Dillydoun Review	"Wasted in a Special Way"
Ethel	"Souls in the Penalty of Flesh"
Gone Lawn	"My Father Sleeps Rough in His Dreams" and "Complexities Run Interference"
Hole in the Head Review	"Hummingbird Feeder"
Live Mag!	"Hotting the Spoon"
MER	"The Crooked Road Without Improvement"
Mollyhouse	"Swim to Shore, Kid"
Moss Trill	"A Vegas Vegan"
New York Quarterly	"Bright-Eyed" and "In My Brain Tonight"
The New Verse News	"It Is Different It Is Not Different"
O You of the Cotton Pajamas! (New Shoreham, Rhode Island: Dusie Press, 2014)	"O You of the Cotton Pajamas!"

Oddball Magazine	"Not Me, It Cries"
Otoliths	"It Is the Body that Gives Us Away" and "Still Not, No"
Peacock Journal	"Three Children Are Laughing"
Pine Hills Review	"Low Life, Malibu" and "How Brilliant Beethoven"
Southampton Review	"The First Time I Had Sex"
Stonewall's Legacy: A Poetry Anthology, eds. Marc Rosen and Rita "Rusty" Rose (Long Island, New York: Local Gems Press, 2019)	"Peril #52 of a Having a Mother," "The Pink Yonder," and "After and Sometimes Stonewall"
Unbroken	"The Shiny You Have Missed"

Set to music by Cornelius Eady, "In My Brain Tonight" was recorded as "My Brain Tonight" by his band, The Cornelius Eady Trio (Cornelius Eady, voice; Lisa Lui, guitar; Charlie Rauh, guitar), in 2023. A track can be found on SoundCloud.

"Three Children Are Laughing" and "Low Life, Malibu" were reprinted online at *The Rainbow Project*. "Low Life, Malibu" was nominated by Poets Wear Prada for a 2024 Pushcart Prize.

Bright-Eyed

Things always work out.

The sun behind you inches up
on autopilot
as when you're at the wheel
and suddenly home wondering:
How did this happen?
Things always work out.
Two feet off the ground,
you face west,
the direction of expansion,
not invention but reinvention
as when you roll out your flesh
cautiously, as if it were
a red carpet subject to inconsideration.
With the East now behind you,
the lush of you spreads
across so much land.
Flips the pages of religion
to the index of nouns.
Thumbs through in search of
a promised earthly garden
of ethereal delight all the while
thanking all that is real.
Thanking all that is real.

Low Life, Malibu

Buoyant and so damn blasé about it,
the ducks are all *You looking at me?*
I can float, *sucker.*

While those puffed-up fighter pilot
gulls straight up sneer, *Haw! Haw!*
fools, we're slumming *it.*

Unhinged as their jaws, they swoop in
on darting fish close to the surface,
then circle our scraps for dessert.

You and me, slouched on wet sand, we
feel the day's chill as a flesh-crawling
parasite. We consider following

the sun as she shimmies down,
searching new and newer horizons,
and each time, we invite her to join us,

up the highway, in a cracked red-
leather booth shaped like a crescent moon.
She might want to but never shows.

We're not big on duty, but we get it.
We have us one responsible sun.
The *I'm-all-that flighty* couldn't care less.

Swim to Shore, Kid

We're all water, mainly,
our mystification floating
above us,
observing us in
the presence of ourselves.
And our mothers.
We are unbearably
substantial
in the wake of
aging's schemed losses
and happenchance
disintegrations.
Yes, it's rough
but life has market value.
The costs of being unseen
pile up like pesos and
Canadian nickels in
a U.S. change purse.
Penalties aplenty
befall the invisible.
Glow, glower, get on with it.
Discombobulate the bores.

A Vegas Vegan

I never promised you a statistician,
although I fantasize on becoming
a poet of actuarial tables,
a poet of the odds, a true Vegas
vegan with an eye keen for
a sun longing for love and,
like a Greek god who mis-
understands the penalties,
melting into the imperishable
west of the sunken and the found.

O You of the Cotton Pajamas!
✈✈✈✈✈✈✈

O you of the cotton pajamas
and frayed bits of life
in your hair every AM!

O niece and nephew,
digging black plastic
picks from Thrifty's
in your do's.

A meteor caromed into
my nephew's sleep.
My sister was with the Navajos.

Wresting fluff and asteroids
from his dreams,
he padded in and, with
the inconsequential body of a
boy, rattled me 'wake.

I settled us one in each bed to
thrash out theology,
Creator's peculiar affections
for us all.

My niece scoped my
acceptability as I daily
handed over sloppy flakes,
and milk in a red-and-white carton.

The backyard. its hangar -ɘ- -ɘ- -ɘ-

7

see the airplane she builds.

Pilot!
Zoom over L.A. puffing
R E M E M B E R
WE ARE LOVED
in Creator's pastel sky!

O you of the cotton pajamas
and frayed bits of life
in your hair every AM!

O niece and nephew,
digging black plastic
picks from Thrifty's
in your do's.

Complexities Run Interference

There are reasons you sign on for years of adult learning and continuing ed sections. *The fool's at it again*, the registrar snickers as a victimy organ near your heart thumps. It thinks it's a rabbit's foot. Think again, unlucky thumper. This life thing is slimy. Hard to get a grip on which does what, Free Will being watermelon-seedy as whim skittering between thumb and forefinger. Once you raced to pay a bill by deadline. Needed polychrome Her. Touchstone. Safe mother. Locked doors opened, and when he came to mop, man, did that Brother jolt. You were accepting of signs. So what if they laugh. Each generation gets hoary and stupid, wants its blunders pyre worthy. Wants the fledglings to learn, lucky thumpers.

Souls in the Penalty of Flesh

The concept of air humming its tune:
girlhood, Bach crooning, un- and happiness,
a consciousness which materialized into her,
the result of an agreement to fuck on Thursdays,
the overpromise of a diaphragm,
immaterial biology and theoretical physics and boom.
We are much too or not enough ignorant of our splendor.
We are souls in the penalty of flesh;
yet by the nectar of flesh, we live in the consciousness
of a girl, twelve, twelve and studying
the ambient inhalation of family.

The Shiny You Have Missed

It is in our nature to teach the two-step, add butter, indulge our pride. We will not rise to our becoming if we are duped by our being, sidetracked by a date of birth, or the whittled praise of a tombstone. Time to explore space, now we are finally out there and in it. Newly mapped fixed points of celestial understanding reveal we are not where we thought we were. No escape from the self. Sins may be original but not pretense, generated during the great resettlements of dust by the systemically unscrupulous. Why are lives not more banal than they are? Join us, my father and me, as we forage the neighborhood to peer through windows of real people homes. So that's what it's like to have a family?

My Father Sleeps Rough in His Dreams

In Burbank we shared a zip code with the quality in Toluca Lake where movie stars lived, Bob Hope and the man who invented Muzak. Pop would write "Toluca Lake" as our return town. At night, I'd sneak into the country club lit by the industrial neon of all that is fantastical about this country, Universal Studio and its parking lot floodlights. My rubber zoris squished grass made spongy by man's design to turn desert into golf course, cool and dewy. Once, a squat man, a mole man, leaned against a shadow holding onto a tree. (The man leaned; the shadow clutched the tree.) His blue jeans were baggy like a movie farmhand's and held up with rope. His face misunderstood. My rubber feet winged it to where Mom sat, reading up on Transcendental coping with Mortal Mind. My father slept rough in his dreams. In some, his brothers scratched "90027" on blue envelopes to be carried, like a lame prince, from New York to California.

The Crooked Road Without Improvement

"... among the most disturbing things to me were the long paved streets."
— Nietzsche, *Jugendschriften*

She is young: a fact which proves nothing.
A twelve-year-old in an abode on the crooked
road without improvement: a strait winding
itself round. The asphalt roar of a cement
mixer churning, the resolve of a chute.
To offset appetites for suburban nostalgia,
think: rats: scurrying: ivy's sprinklered
banks *before* the house, *before* as in:
I trembled *before* the hanging judge, so
trembled ivy before the squatting house.
No rats in the house squatting atop the bank.
We die absolved at the end: roads, you, me.

It Is the Body that Gives Us Away

"Prepare yourself for the moonship journey" — Sun Ra

The gigantic character cannot
live as other than herself,
you will agree someday
Without a container
where are freedoms safe?

Great respect for old-time fags
Youngs! Do you even know?

What to grab when you take off
Another century we will see her as she was
A female body is a fact
flesh its fortune

Oh but   skin

Sandra Bernhard in *The King of Comedy*:
"I want to be Black"
<the desperation of my race>

It is the body that gives us away
The messengers are free of degradation

>>>Churches are burning in the South<<<

Take off, Soul
Problems of bodies are for the living
Problems of hell for the living and dead

Still Not, No

That shit wasn't easy
They still haven't
white civil rightsers
moved to the Crenshaw District
Samuel who was Peter to us
Pete to be Pete
Samuel to be Black
Peter to be brother-in-law
Man, you were twelve
when that sister married
The actualization of a you
            not in sight
Being a purist is often
a losing thing   an imaginary
Nature learns on the job:
blueprints mess with us
Evolution of the ignorants is
            nowhere really
Bullies bust us open
The hard road turns us into saviors
            Pete to be Pete
            Sam to be himself
To have a self
That's an art

Two-Story Bldg. on Vernon

"But when it comes to funking it up, Groove had no match."
— Jürgen Wolf

It is Sunday.
Richard "Groove" Holmes lives upstairs.
He gets his own poem.
Her sister et al. are downstairs.
Groove is big-bellied.
You know big-bellied men,
How solid big bellies can be.
That was him at the electric organ.
"After Hours."
He's left his apartment now and
descended the stairway for
California sun.
Air about his body more so.
His body more so.
Is how it is with well knowns.
The more so.
Richard "Groove" Holmes's squint
inquires of her psyche.
The particular flattery of an adult.
This thirteen-year-old
Balancing on crabgrass.
Thirteen and white.
Her brother-in-law black.
Late afternoon, the family
drive back to the Valley.
That new sound everyone
heard is not on the radio.

How Brilliant Beethoven

If my father believed he needed to arm himself against the insanely damaged carrying rapid-fire to end everyday schoolkids with still-squishy bodies perfecting daffy walks or teens with their dreams of endless horizons after high school, some part of them knowing life doesn't give up on its challenge but that youth is a superpower. Well, if my father owned a gun, he'd have fumbled opening the safe, shouted at my mom and sisters to be careful as he lifted a lockbox from the safe, trembled working the lockbox, and shaken on realizing nothing left to open but a box of bullets and opening that would call the question. He'd have howled there was no locked box in the lockbox in the safe, not that we ever owned a safe or lockbox to lock in it, insisted we were moving back to New York. My mother, who was Christian, would have taken gun and bullets from his twitching hand to load the pistol. She gave birth four times and also could drown mice in the toilet or a pail of water. She would not have shot anyone, would have denied the weapon existed, then read Bible and attendant texts while my father, calmed by a shot of whiskey, demanded to know if I had read Robert Louis Stevenson yet, and if me and my three sisters, each far older than I will ever be, had a clue how brilliant Beethoven was.

Hotting the Spoon

Our central shared memory
on Southern California's
          contrived lawns:
Mom and the bee.

Judee watched her halt one,
U-turn it buzzy in flight.

To the bee's Truth,
Mom spoke
transcendentally.
I watched Judee watch Mom.

My sister was arrested
for being a hippie in Texas.
Mom concentrated the weather.
A hurricane slammed the Lone Star State.
Where Judee was then?

In London with the Kinks?
At Dale's in the flats of Hollywood?
In a house thrumming with albums?

Death is a spiritual reorganization.
Mom tried to overcome flesh.
We are all immortal.
Judee Sill then; and now.

Finery in the Aisles

I wish you the gift of letting go.
I wish I remembered learning it years ago.
I wish you knew time moves faster than pain
and in the lapse
memories stretch
so thin we don't recognize them
for what they are
                        (which is)
            the past come begging.
I wish that were true and nothing's
            held but for
            a grudge that
                        motivates.

Not Me, It Cries

My past doesn't haunt me.
I haunt my past.
In the middle of the night, it jerks 'wake:
"Shit. Now what're you gonna blame me for?"
Spots my darkened eye,
my smile a loop, a cache of memories
tooling outskirts of best times ever,
gone days, manic when manic
was friends who could spot
a grand weirdness of bravery,
originality manifested.
Youth is now cringe-worthy.
"I don't know why that's gone,"
my past cries, confused
about age's clarity

Peril #52 of a Having a Mother

Alois talked up
fastidious habits he
observed while engaged
in love's excitations.
Bus drivers on Haight
were clued in, shop clerks,
everyone in a radius knew
his pride of ownership.

I wish Mom talked sex
as much as he did.
I know lots about travels of the spirit.
I'm sort of mental.

May I take off my clothes.
That's a prayer.
May I take off my clothes,
roll about and know the cloud of unknowing.
Sweetie, it wants to be known, don't you think?

The First Time I Had Sex

The first time I had sex
was followed by
the second time I had sex.
Not the same night,
not the same locale.
The first time I had sex
was in a dorm room
on a twin mattress with
a boy needing to believe
he was fucking for mercy
from whoever it was
in his fair youth, who
held his fair youth
in a fist and crushed.
The first time I had sex
was fine in the done-
and-done sense. He said,
"Now you're a woman."
I thought, *Not your call.*
The second time I had
sex I don't remember.
Somewhere. Scattered
bedrooms, motels,
Pasadena, Silverlake Sunset.
One penis too big, another
so small I felt his terror.
I chose a piano player at a bar.
The man who gave me
the clap chose me.
I made out with a woman in
her car idling on a hill.
The emergency brake was

worrisome, but her mouth was
smooth as familiar sheets
welcoming me every night.
Dang, I was afraid.
There's a moral here and it is:
Don't be afraid.
Sex with men wasn't awful.
Sex with women, floral
in the night and leathery.
The moral here:
Our bodies are soft foothills
in spring. The sun sends
its warmth to grass greening
on soft foothills in spring.

The Pink Yonder

        some of us pining to meet
state-of-the-art girls
        almighty love
        ever-expansive dewdrop rainbow

other hippie chick handles

        mint-condition girls
        playing their hand

           shuffling a deck
hid up their sleeve of many cards

girls loose with freedoms
        the ones in the gift bag
        yielded to us when we were
        sprung from our jail cell

you know the one.

did Judee know I was queer?

After and Sometimes Stonewall

Relive those parties where every bottle was uncorked and
passed around, and everyone smoked everything, double-
checked each auto's glove box for at least a Sherman or
a roach. And you left with exactly the wrong woman who
was exactly the right one, if only for less than twelve hours.
And not everyone was anything, not white, employed,
focused. And all had self-righteous halos of wild hair
imperfect as a precisely imprecise stitch in a Persian rug.

No One's in High School These Days

We graduate with contrastive badges,
weirdo girl, prom girl, high-IQ girl,
neutral girl in the bleachers one row
behind puffy coat-wearing skinny
page-girl girl next to goofy boy
jabbing her car coat's loft, *pow,*
pow, right index finger, *pow pow*,
left index finger, lipping, *You look*
fat in this coat, *pow*, and neutral girl
thinking *Shut up* and skinny page-
girl girl thinking, *She'll skip the coat*
next week, nerdy girl, abused girl,
abused girl, abused girl, pot-dealing
girl, acid-dropping girl, girl who in
seventy years will be not-so-bitter
girl, immovable-past girl, future girl.

In a Yard in Southern California

A paradise, a heckle,
a lemon-blossom goad,
a prickly schematic,
spiny and needle-riven.
All that and not enough.
Jasmine-reeling night dis-
solves in the yard's innate
abeyance to life, the lawn
ever prostrate beneath sun's
streaming zeal half on
half off. Simple yards
made fitting by light,
broker sidewalk, and house-
push assimilation of
purpose — a compliance
with destinies shared by
the accident of a stretch
of parched dirt and grass.
By this, habitation
and sidewalk are joined.
We leave for new
geographies, but the in-
between connector
house — yard yard — sidewalk
assures the lost, the sullen.

Patio-Speak

This Poem is
an   exploration of
          the fallacy of
          indoor-outdoor furniture
pursuant to
duck droppings on a
          squeaking two-seater
          with
weather-rent plastic cushions
          clawed by
          feral Huey Lord One-Eye
who is on her seventh life,
per general sentiment.   So.
Three of us drag the
Adirondack chair from inside to,
          I am thinking, *the deck!*
          But there isn't one so
we settle it on
          a concrete patch
          to surveil snails and
the overhead, stars, the vault
          unplugged.
Significance?
          Examine your life
          worth living.
          You'll be sat on night
and day if you stay in
or sat on beneath
the reeling ecstasy
if you are out. Nothing
          is easy except hiding
          which is

crack cocaine cut with angel dust.
It'll destroy you quick.

Bright-Eyed

The past is over, and that happens more than you think. Which could be speculation like *They don't fire him because they don't know we know or don't care we know or academic freedom is a privilege but not like we thought.* Memory is unreliable, making misdirection the sticker price of retrospection. The value of the past being how it orients instinct. *Hey. Holiness went that way?* Your co-workers raided the dispensary. The shrink wrote you a scrip for Valium. The pain center was a tumor crazy for your right ovary. Read the sign and calculate a likelihood, lovable odds you'll self-spiritualize. That cerebellum zone passed on by your father helms navigationally precise insight, codifying you and him as a teensy admirable and weensily intimidating. Look to your future. It's malleable, not like ducklings, more like wet clay shivering in anticipation of thumbs. Unreliable memory is understudy for sublimity. Observation and waiting, a daily workout. Zero in on the thing bright-eyed and hopping with *more.*

Wasted in a Special Way

She stopped the car on Beverly and ordered
everyone out into an evening cooled by
City of Angels' angels winging in
from confabs with other angels.
From gossip. Angels love chat.

One angel's crossed leg over another's.
Aloft on white puffies, smoking.
Everyone ordered out of the car to
          march around the car.
I am she who orders.

The Chevy became a prophet's tomb,
Rumi's sacred bower
trembling branches cedar.
Giddy canyons of stored sun
wait a distance closer than Vegas,
a distance mappable.

It was good to be young and loaded,
to shape the air condensed with
Great Mother's tears.
To hide out in the good fortune of
a safe ride home where fates tangled to
windy rhythms of snores from
beasts almost tamed.

It is always good to be young and loaded.
Something, somewhere is always good.
Something, somewhere is always wasted.

It Is Different It Is Not Different

40 mug shots of
Freedom Riders

arrested 24 May
1961 and jailed

Jackson
Mississippi.

John Lewis is
third from right

top row.
CT Vivian second

row
second from left.

In
Louisville KY

435 mug shots
of

as many protestors
jailed

saying her
name

(Breonna
Taylor)

are not yet
released.

Add 400
more

Freedom Riders.
I can't

find them
all

Those solid
of will.

Big Little Lambs

My nephew and niece,
half-white all-Black,
don't care about my divided self,
my split-at-the-rootness,
Christian blah blah Jewish blah blah.
White + white is two whites
spooning in a pudding of white.
With all respect to my folks.
Hey, I know Black is not
for sure saintly as most saints
are not for sure saintly.
But for their time on the rack.
Let's rest this poem on an oven
rack, as if it were lamb led
to dinner, a lamb dripping with
blood, connection, and shame.
This poem is heliocentric as
the ego basking in itself.
Nephew and niece, they grow,
as we're said to in California,
sprouting leaf after shiny leaf
happy as neon or sundrops.
Erin thanked me for the fifty!
Come on. Sing Happy Birthday.

Some Mysteries of Youth Unsolved
(Where I Lived When I Was 13)

rats lay low in ivy,
a wet bank of it,
the leveling up of a slope
straining for your house
wrapped in scrim.

snaking ivy.
childhood on pivots.
there exist taxonomies
of four-walled habitats
to explore never fully.

however you figure,
each thieving pin eye's
a lighthouse of rapacity.
rats ferret ivy, searching
cores, grinding, paring

the refuse of hope.
lives reenact contorted
memory, reenactment being
a distortion, a cry, and
even now, a question.

Hummingbird Feeder

What is the value of having a soul,
that however-defined sensory intelligence
prompting us to
become a flank of stars or
huddle of trees?
For one,
the soul is not a people.
For one,
the soul does not do terrible things.
The self? Destroy it.
Step outside.
Top off the hummingbird feeder.
Less time to be terrible.
Less time to judge.
Them, us, yourself.
For one, for honor, for a lark.

Three Children Are Laughing

They fall and float up —
the ocean, deep space, the moon.
They were not issued boots.
They don't care. They are gone.
They wear taffetas, twinsets,
garlands of sorrow strung on ivory,
eat five grams of Cheerios
every ten years if that is what they
need to count tulips, ochers
of the dust we once thought
was all there was to life.

In My Brain Tonight

All the kids are partying in my brain tonight
Mom, everyone's having fun in my brain tonight
Me too I'm getting loaded in my brain tonight
All relaxed and marinating in my brain tonight
Not attached to any promise of my brain tonight
No pleasure-prissies in my brain tonight
Hella mamas hella tunes in my brain tonight
Geneva Convention conventioneers wild
Conventioneering in my brain tonight and sure
Tomorrow creeps in but nothing in my brain
Tonight is petty not in this brain not tonight

Acknowledgments

I am grateful beyond words to Poets Wear Prada Press, especially to Roxanne Hoffman of Hoboken, New Jersey, for her boundless energy, enthusiasm, and expertise, and to Jack Cooper, of Paris, France, for his keen-eyed editing. Whew. You two are patient.

Thanks to an assortment of New York poets I haven't been able to scare off, including Amy Holman, Brad Vogel, Cornelius Eady, Jane Ormerod, Jee Leong Koh, Jiwon Choi, Linda Kleinbub, Mackenzie Carnigan, Michael Broder, and Su Polo, among them.

Finally, love to my genius family, all Californian, all the time: Erin, Evan, and René; Arely, Cael, Esai, and Mark. You are the warmest, funniest, most talented, most generous folks around.

— SARAH SARAI

About the Author

Sarah Sarai is the author of several poetry collections including *That Strapless Bra in Heaven* (Kelsay Books, 2019); *Geographies of Soul and Taffeta* (Indolent Books, 2016); and *The Future Is Happy* (BlazeVOX Books, 2009). Her poems are widely anthologized, most notably in Gerald LaFemina's *Composing Poetry, a Guide to Writing Poems and Thinking Lyrically* (Kendall Hunt Publishing, 2016) and *Say It Loud: Poems About James Brown*, edited by Michael Oatman and Mary Weems (Whirlwind Press, 2011). A native New Yorker, born in Long Island, she grew up in Los Angeles and studied at St. Johns College in Santa Fe, before returning to attend Sarah Lawrence College, where she earned her MFA in Writing. Her honors include a fellowship from the National Endowment for the Humanities and grants from both the Seattle and the King County Arts Commissions. Her ekphrastic poem "Promises Had Been Made," after *The Entombment* by Moretto de Besco, was the first place, cash prize winner of the 2017 PersonalLordSaviorJesusChrist Poetry Contest sponsored by Chris Rice Cooper's blog and judged by Helen Losse. Ms. Sarai wrote some poetry aboard the sailboat *Nellie Bly*, in April of 2023, as part of NYC Poets Afloat, a poetry micro-residency and reading series organized by Brad Vogel in conjunction with National Poetry Month, which culminated in a June reading on the Waterfront Museum barge in Red Hook, Brooklyn. She currently lives in New York City and works as an independent editor.

A NOTE ON THE TYPE

This book is set in Minion Pro, an Old-Style serif typeface designed by Robert Slimbach of Adobe Systems, and released in 1990 by Linotype. Inspired by the mass-produced publications of the late Renaissance, but with a contemporary crispness and clarity not possible with the print machinery of that era, even by the best of the Renaissance typographers, this modern-day interpretation is well regarded for its classic baroque-rooted styling and its enhanced legibility. One of the five or six most widely used typefaces for trade paperback fiction published in the United States over the past several years, Minion Pro is the typeface adopted by the Smithsonian for its logo. The name Minion is derived from the traditional classification and nomenclature of typeface sizes; *minion*, the size between *brevier* and *nonpareil*, approximates a modern 7-point lettering size.

www.ingramcontent.com/pod-product-compliance
Lightning Source LLC
Chambersburg PA
CBHW031935080426
42734CB00007B/698